Sister, Tell me your story...

101 Questions For Your Sister To Share Her Life And Thoughts

What is your full name, birthdate, and where were you born?

_____

_____

_____

_____

_____

_____

_____

_____

_____

_____

_____

_____

_____

_____

_____

_____

_____

_____

_____

_____

Were you named after anyone?
Did you have any nicknames as a child?

Where did you go to grammar school, high school, and college?

_____

_____

_____

_____

_____

_____

_____

_____

_____

_____

_____

_____

_____

_____

_____

_____

_____

_____

_____

_____

What are the earliest memories of your first home?
What about other places you lived?

What do you remember most about your parents?

What were the occupations of your parents?

What were your favorite toys and games as a kid?

What were some things that your mom or dad always said to you when you were young?

Did you ever collect anything as a kid?

What did you want to be when you grew up?

_____

_____

_____

_____

_____

_____

_____

_____

_____

_____

_____

_____

_____

_____

_____

_____

_____

_____

_____

What do you remember about your grandparents?

_____

_____

_____

_____

_____

_____

_____

_____

_____

_____

_____

_____

_____

_____

_____

_____

_____

_____

_____

Do you remember your grandparents
describing their lives?
What did they say?

_____

_____

_____

_____

_____

_____

_____

_____

_____

_____

_____

_____

_____

_____

_____

_____

_____

_____

_____

_____

_____

_____

What did your family do for fun when you were a kid?

_____

_____

_____

_____

_____

_____

_____

_____

_____

_____

_____

_____

_____

_____

_____

_____

_____

_____

_____

What was the neighborhood like where you grew up?

What kind of chores did you do as a kid? Did you get an allowance?

_____

_____

_____

_____

_____

_____

_____

_____

_____

_____

_____

_____

_____

_____

_____

_____

_____

_____

What do you remember most about your father?

_____
_____
_____
_____
_____
_____
_____
_____
_____
_____
_____
_____
_____
_____
_____
_____
_____
_____
_____
_____
_____
_____

What do you remember most about your mother?

_____
_____
_____
_____
_____
_____
_____
_____
_____
_____
_____
_____
_____
_____
_____
_____
_____
_____
_____
_____
_____

Who was your best friend as a child?

What are some of your memories of your brothers and sisters?

Did you and your friends have a special place to hang out?

Did you ever do anything naughty?

Were there any subjects or teachers you particularly liked or disliked at school?

What was the most foolish thing you did as a kid?

Were you involved in any school sports or clubs?
Did you receive any awards?

Did you have a job during high school?

How would people who knew you in high school describe you?

What family trips do you remember most?

What do you remember most about your teenage years?

Who was your best friend in high school?

Who was your first date with, and what was it like?

What family recipes do you remember as a kid?

What comes to mind when you think about growing up in your hometown?

What did a typical Friday night look like for you at age seventeen?

What was your first car?

What was your first job?
How much money did you make?

What did you like to do in high school?

What things did you wear in high school?

What did you do after high school?

What advice did your parents give you?

How did you meet your spouse?

When was the moment you realized you wanted to marry your spouse?

_____

_____

_____

_____

_____

_____

_____

_____

_____

_____

_____

_____

_____

_____

_____

_____

_____

_____

_____

_____

_____

_____

What was your wedding like?

Did you have a honeymoon?
Where did you go?

_____

_____

_____

_____

_____

_____

_____

_____

_____

_____

_____

_____

_____

_____

_____

_____

_____

_____

_____

_____

_____

_____

_____

Do you have any advice about marriage?

_____

_____

_____

_____

_____

_____

_____

_____

_____

_____

_____

_____

_____

_____

_____

_____

_____

_____

Why did you name your children what you did?

_____
_____
_____
_____
_____
_____
_____
_____
_____
_____
_____
_____
_____
_____
_____
_____
_____
_____
_____
_____
_____

Were you ever scared to be a parent?

What did it feel like to have children?

What do you remember about when each of your children was born?

What qualities of your children are most like you?

What qualities of your children are most like their father?

What are three words that represent your approach to parenting and why?

_____

_____

_____

_____

_____

_____

_____

_____

_____

_____

_____

_____

_____

_____

_____

_____

_____

_____

_____

_____

Is there any day as a parent you wish you could do over again?

Are there any funny or unusual things you remember your children doing?

What is the most essential element of being a good mother?

Did you serve in the military?
Did any other family members serve in the military?

Are you happy with the career you chose?
What would you do for work if you could
do it over again?

Have you won any special awards or prizes as an adult?
What were they for?

_____

_____

_____

_____

_____

_____

_____

_____

_____

_____

_____

_____

_____

_____

_____

_____

_____

_____

_____

_____

_____

What made you successful at work?

What organizations or groups have you been a member of?

Have you met any famous people?

How many times have you been in love?

If you could have dinner with three famous people, living or dead, who would they be and why?

_____

_____

_____

_____

_____

_____

_____

_____

_____

_____

_____

_____

_____

_____

_____

_____

_____

_____

_____

_____

Is there anything you would do differently in life if you knew what you know now?

_____

_____

_____

_____

_____

_____

_____

_____

_____

_____

_____

_____

_____

_____

_____

_____

_____

_____

_____

_____

_____

_____

Was there a person who really impacted the course of your life?

_____

_____

_____

_____

_____

_____

_____

_____

_____

_____

_____

_____

_____

_____

_____

_____

_____

_____

_____

_____

_____

_____

Was there a defining moment that helped
you grow into the person you are today?

What historical event in your lifetime had the most impact on you?

What activities have you enjoyed as an adult?

What advice would you give your 20-year-old self?

What are you most thankful for?

Who and what are your favorite singers, bands, songs, movies, and books?

What do you believe people want the most in life?

What do you think are the most significant inventions in your lifetime?

_____

_____

_____

_____

_____

_____

_____

_____

_____

_____

_____

_____

_____

_____

_____

_____

_____

_____

_____

_____

_____

_____

What do you think the world needs more of right now?

What do you wish you could ask your parents?

What has become more important to you over time?

What has been your favorite age so far, and why?

What have been the happiest moments of your life?

What have been the saddest moments of your life?

What is one message you want to tell your grandkids?

_____
_____
_____
_____
_____
_____
_____
_____
_____
_____
_____
_____
_____
_____
_____
_____
_____
_____

What is something you've never told anyone else before?

What is something you're very proud of?

What is the funniest family story you remember?

_____

_____

_____

_____

_____

_____

_____

_____

_____

_____

_____

_____

_____

_____

_____

_____

_____

_____

What is the most beautiful place you have ever visited, and what was it like?

_____
_____
_____
_____
_____
_____
_____
_____
_____
_____
_____
_____
_____
_____
_____
_____
_____
_____
_____
_____
_____

Do you believe in ghosts or extraterrestrials?

What musical instruments do you wish you knew how to play?

What makes you laugh more than anything?

What message would you like to share with your family?

_____

_____

_____

_____

_____

_____

_____

_____

_____

_____

_____

_____

_____

_____

_____

_____

_____

_____

_____

_____

What pets have you had? Tell me about them.

What states have you visited? What countries have you visited?

What three events most shaped your life?

_____

_____

_____

_____

_____

_____

_____

_____

_____

_____

_____

_____

_____

_____

_____

_____

_____

_____

_____

_____

_____

_____

What was the funniest practical joke you ever played on someone?

Do you believe in a Higher Power?

What were the three best decisions you ever made?

What were the hardest choices you ever made?

What's one underrated but essential skill a person should possess?

What's the best gift you've ever received?

What keeps you awake at night?

If you could go back and change one significant experience in your life, what would it be and why?

Who are your closest friends?
Who is your oldest friend?

Are you where you thought you'd be at this point in your life?

How do you want to be remembered?